THE STORY OF HANUKKAH

Paintings by ORI SHERMAN

THE STORY OF HANUKKAH

told by AMY EHRLICH

A Puffin Pied Piper

PUFFIN PIED PIPER BOOKS
Published by the Penguin Group
Penguin Books USA Inc., 375 Hudson Street, New York, New York 10014, U.S.A.
Penguin Books Ltd, 27 Wrights Lane, London W8 5TZ, England
Penguin Books Australia Ltd, Ringwood, Victoria, Australia
Penguin Books Canada Ltd, 10 Alcorn Avenue, Toronto, Ontario, Canada M4V 3B2
Penguin Books (N.Z.) Ltd, 182-190 Wairau Road, Auckland 10, New Zealand
Penguin Books Ltd, Registered Offices: Harmondsworth, Middlesex, England

Originally published in hardcover by
Dial Books
A Division of Penguin Books USA Inc.

Library of Congress Catalog Card Number: 88-31109
Printed in the U.S.A.
First Puffin Pied Piper Printing 1994
ISBN 0-14-055285-5

1 3 5 7 9 10 8 6 4 2

THE STORY OF HANUKKAH
is also published in hardcover editions by
Dial Books.

Pictured on the frontispiece is a dreidel, a four-sided spinning top. On each side is a Hebrew letter: nun (N), gimmel (G), heh (H), shin (SH). They stand for the Hebrew words *Nes, Gadol, Hayah, Sham,* which mean "A Great Miracle Happened There." On the nights of Hanukkah children play with the top, winning small prizes such as nuts, raisins, or pennies.

The art for this book was created using gouache, a painting technique in which opaque colors are ground in water and mixed with a preparation of gum. Each painting was then color-separated and reproduced in full color.

For my grandnieces, Rachael and Heather

O. S.

For Aunt Ida and Cousin Johnny

A. E.

Long ago in the ancient land of Judea, the Jews dwelt in peace. They wanted only to worship God, to keep His laws, and to celebrate His glory.

Their temple in the holy city of Jerusalem stood on Mount Moriah for all to see. Within its walls were many precious objects, but among them was a simple lamp. For hundreds of years the Jews had kept it burning. Its strong, clear light showed the power of their faith.

In those days a king named Alexander reigned over the Jews, and he was merciful. But it happened that another who was called Antiochus came into the land. With a multitude of soldiers he came to Jerusalem and decreed that the Jews must forsake their laws. No longer could they keep the Sabbath or worship God in their temple. Now the Jews must bow down before idols and if any refused, they would die.

While faithful Jews watched in horror, the soldiers entered the temple itself. They placed an idol upon the golden altar and allowed pigs to run there. They drank from the holy vessels, and then they set fire to the books of the law.

The oil in the lamp was spilled and the light in the temple went out.

Now, in the town of Modin there dwelt a man called Mattathias, who had five sons. And when they saw what had been done to the temple of Jerusalem, they wept and mourned sorely. Never, they vowed, would they forsake God's laws.

The king's soldiers came and set an idol in the town, but Mattathias threw it down and called to the people, saying, "Whoever is for the Lord, come." Then he and his sons fled into the mountains, and many who sought justice also followed.

When the king was told that the Jews had gone down into the wilderness, he assembled a vast army. It was the Sabbath and the Jews were forbidden to fight.

But soldiers rose up in battle against them, slaughtering thousands. Then the Jews saw that they must fight even on the Sabbath.

One day Mattathias died and his son Judah the Maccabee led the Jews, for he was a great warrior. But the people were frightened and came to Judah, saying, "How can we who are so few fight against a multitude?"

That night under the starry sky Judah prayed to God, and when morning came he said to the people, "Do not be afraid, for the Lord is with us. Strength comes from heaven, it is not in the size of an army."

Then valiantly the Jews fought, defeating all the armies and generals that Antiochus could send against them. But when they marched triumphantly into Jerusalem and saw the temple abandoned and desolate, the strong soldiers began to weep.

Then Judah and those who were with him went up to cleanse the temple. They built the altar again according to the law and made new holy vessels and other precious things. At last it was time to light the lamp and rededicate the temple to God.

They searched all the rooms and courtyards until they found one cruse of pure oil the invaders had overlooked. But it was enough for only a day.

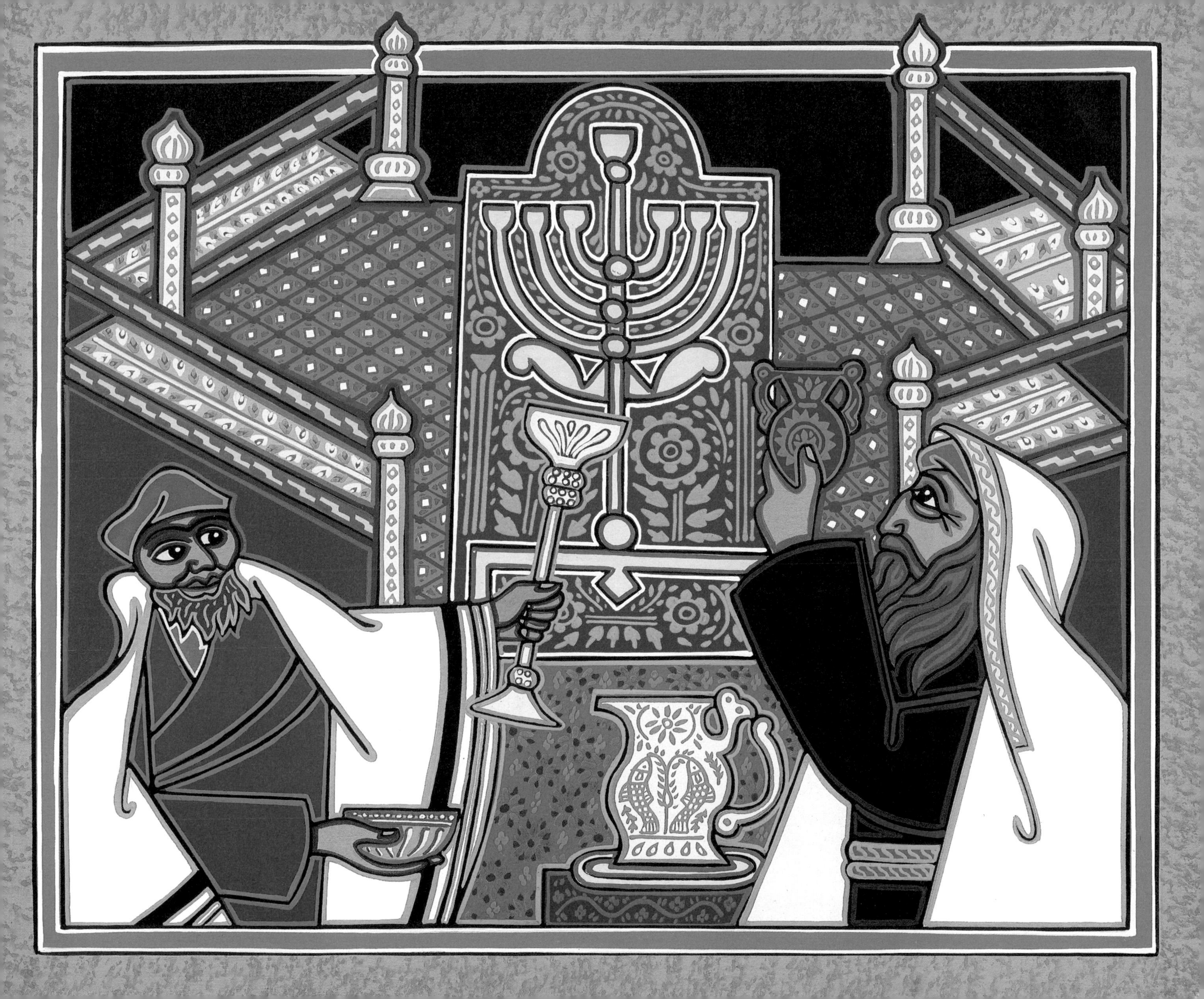

And after Judah saw this he took the cruse of oil in his hand and said to the people, "Let us yet rejoice in what we have and light the lamp to worship and praise God who has delivered us."

Then the people fell upon their knees and prayed.

They thought it would burn for only a day, but the oil in the lamp kept burning. Some said the flame grew brighter and brighter, illuminating every corner of the temple and dazzling the worshippers at their prayers.

And when more pure oil was finally made, the oil had burned for eight days and eight nights.

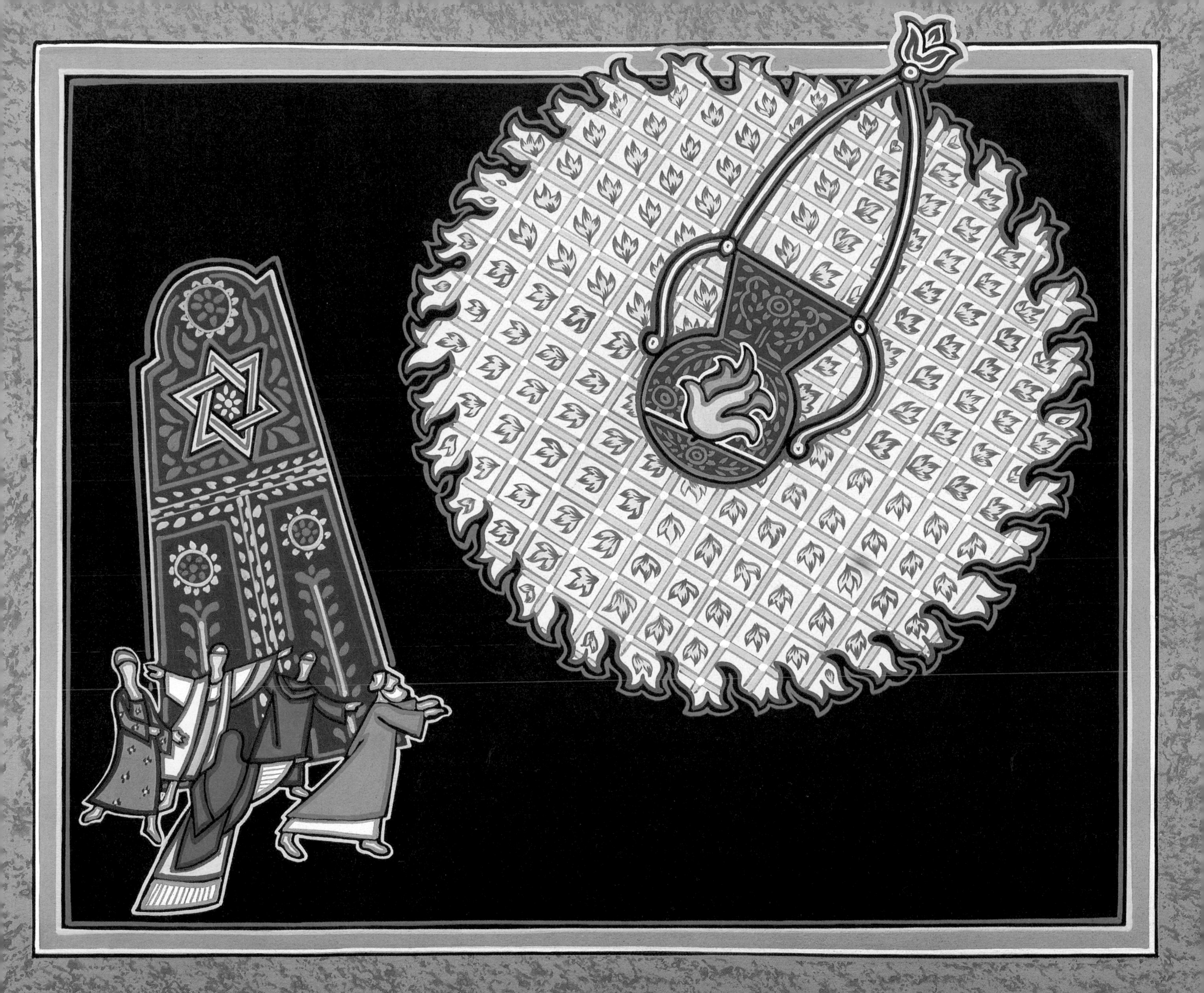

These events were in the Hebrew month of Kislev, beginning on the twenty-fifth day. Afterward Judah and his brothers decreed that the eight days of the rededication of the temple should be kept always in their season from year to year.

And so, like the oil of long ago, the lights of Hanukkah still burn brightly, proclaiming God's glory and the freedom of the Jews.

Amy Ehrlich

is the author of many books for children, including the Leo, Zack, and Emmie Easy-to-Read books with illustrations by Steven Kellogg. Her retellings of classic fairy tales include *Cinderella, The Snow Queen, Thumbelina,* and *The Wild Swans,* all illustrated by Susan Jeffers; and *Rapunzel* with pictures by Kris Waldherr. Ms. Ehrlich's first novel, *Where It Stops, Nobody Knows* (Dial), received the 1990 Dorothy Canfield Fisher Award and was cited by *Booklist* as a Best of the Decade book. Her most recent books include *Lucy's Winter Tale,* illustrated by Troy Howell, which *Kirkus* called "intriguing"; and *Parents in the Pigpen, Pigs in the Tub,* illustrated by Steven Kellogg, which *Publishers Weekly* called "a Thanksgiving dinner, filled with extra helpings of silliness." Ms. Ehrlich lives on a farm in Vermont.

Ori Sherman

was born in Jerusalem and emigrated with his family to New York when he was three years old. Before his untimely death Mr. Sherman was an exhibiting fine artist in a variety of media—paper, wood, fabric, and metal, though he found some of his greatest joy in the art of illustrating picture books.